Be One of the Lucky Ones

Be One of the Lucky Ones

* *

A Specialty Doctors' Guide to Financial Freedom and Peace of Mind

Anthony C. Williams, ChFC, RFC, CLU, CLTC

And

Marc E. Ortega, ChFC, RFC, CLTC

iUniverse, Inc.
New York Lincoln Shanghai

Be One of the Lucky Ones
A Specialty Doctors' Guide to Financial Freedom and Peace of Mind

iUniverse books may be ordered through booksellers or by contacting:

iUniverse
2021 Pine Lake Road, Suite 100
Lincoln, NE 68512
www.iuniverse.com
1-800-Authors (1-800-288-4677)

The information, ideas, and suggestions in this book are not intended to render professional advice. Before following any suggestions contained in this book, you should consult your personal accountant or other financial advisor. Neither the author nor the publisher shall be liable or responsible for any loss or damage allegedly arising as a consequence of your use or application of any information or suggestions in this book.

ISBN: 978-0-595-43913-3 (pbk)
ISBN: 978-0-595-88235-9 (ebk)

Printed in the United States of America

Contents

Thank You

A personal note of thanks goes to several people. Thanks to our clients who provided feedback and ultimately asked the question, "Is there anything we can read about this stuff?" Thank you to Sheila Evans and Bonita MacFarland for their input, guidance, and editing. Thank you to our mentors, without whom none of this would be possible. Finally, a huge thanks goes to our wives for enduring our time away while working on this project.

Foreword

by P. Shaun McDuffee, CLU, ChFC, AEP

When Anthony and Marc asked me to write a Forward for their book I immediately accepted. I have the privilege of knowing the two of them since 1994. The book you are about to read is filled with no-nonsense advice garnered from a dozen years of experience in working with specialty doctors. Consider this book a handy reference guide, to not only make you aware of common pitfalls doctors face, but also ideas on how to alleviate those challenges.

> ## Our Mission Statement
>
> **We help specialty doctors and their families with strategies designed to create and protect wealth in order to provide financial freedom and peace of mind.**

I

Introduction

If you are like most specialty doctors, your time is at a premium. You have spent the majority of your young adult life in school and in training. After eight to twelve years of learning your specialty, the time has come to enter the professional workforce and enjoy the fruits of your labor.

Your future income will provide great opportunity but also some significant challenges. In our experience, the time our clients have spent in their medical training often leaves them ill-equipped to deal with personal and professional financial situations. These challenges generally lead clients down the path of anxiety, agitation, and playing catch up; often those emotions crossing over into their personal lives. Most of our clients have asked questions pertaining to these challenges such as:

1. Is my family protected from personal and/or professional lawsuit?
2. What happens if I can no longer earn an income?
3. How much do I need to retire?
4. When should I start saving or investing?
5. What is the best way to develop a savings/investing plan?
6. Who should I look to for advice?
7. I rotated with someone who says he will never retire. What can I do so that won't happen to me?
8. How can I think about these issues while shouldering debt?
9. How much should I spend on a home?
10. Of which types of benefits should I be aware?

These are only a few of the questions we have been asked, there are far too many to list here. The purpose of this book is to provide general guidance as a resource for specialty doctors as they seek financial independence.

The question then becomes, "Are YOU one of the lucky ones?" Yes! We feel you can become "lucky" with deliberate forward-thinking and planning. You can sleep well at night knowing that you have taken steps to protect yourself and your family if tragedy strikes. You will know you are on the path towards achieving your financial objectives.

Now, begin your journey to become one of the Lucky Ones.

II

Why Now?

A. Over the past ten years of our professional practices along with research and consultation with many specialty doctors, we came to one dramatic conclusion: many of our clients suffer from IDILS. Unfortunately, there is no pill for I'll Do It Later Syndrome. Often, depending on the individuals' personal or professional status, we hear the following:

1. "I'm in training now; I'll start looking at these issues closer to the end of my training."
2. "I'm too busy finishing training and interviewing. I'll start evaluating these issues when I get into practice and have money."
3. "I just started practice and have too much going on now; once I become a partner will be a better time."
4. "I'm single; these issues are irrelevant to me until I get married."
5. "We just got married and are too busy; we can wait to address these issues until we have children."

B. If people wait until they are several years into practice to begin the planning process (especially after partnership is achieved) the following things will happen:

1. They will continue to put off planning.
2. They will constantly feel behind.
3. They will increase their standard of living to meet or exceed their income ceiling.

4.   The likelihood of achieving their goals decreases.
5.   They may not achieve peace of mind regarding their financial situation.

In fact, one of the primary reasons we began speaking at teaching hospitals throughout the western United States is because our clients continually expressed to us the following: "I wish I had looked into these issues earlier. If I had, I would now be much further ahead than I am and probably wouldn't have made so many mistakes." They would then ask us to speak at the institution where they completed training; as well as to their colleagues at their existing practices.

The bottom line, however, is that there is a treatment for IDILS: the earlier you begin the planning process; you improve your chances for achieving your financial goals and objectives.

What is luck?

The definition we use is *"when opportunity meets preparation."* Personally, we do not believe in luck. You may ask then, "Why write a book about being one of the lucky ones?" The answer is to demonstrate that you and you alone control the luck factor using our definition. Through your determination, motivation, and planning you will be more likely to achieve your financial objectives, goals, and dreams.

A.   Okay, if we have the definition of luck in place, let's break down the two components. First, the **opportunity**. How many people do you know who can expect to transition from $40,000 per year in income to $200,000 or more? With this type of income increase, your opportunity is your ability to lay the foundation of your financial plan prior to establishing or increasing your standard of living. When you take a proactive approach to your planning anticipating the income increase your likelihood of success increases tremendously.

B.   Next, what are the steps involved in the **preparation**? Here are the thirteen steps.

   1.   **Identify Your Goals and Objectives.**
        You have likely heard about the power of visualization. When it comes to goal setting, it is well proven that people who visualize and write specific goals for their futures are more likely to achieve their goals, and obtain higher net worth than those who do not.

2.   **Review Your Budget.**
     While in training, most doctors work on a cash-in cash-out environment. When reviewing your budget you will find areas of opportunity as a result of unnecessary spending. Additionally, it prepares you to turn your budget upside down. In other words, determine what your goals are and what they will cost, and adjust your expenses or standard of living accordingly. Pay yourself first is an expression supporting this idea of allocating monies to your goals first and then towards your standard of living.

3.   **Determine Children's College Education Funding.** Spouses' differing perspectives often result in disagreement about planning for education costs. For example, Anthony and his wife Wendy, come from very different backgrounds; she from an extremely affluent family, and he from a middle-class family. As such, when they discussed having children and funding their education, it took some time to find agreement. Wendy wanted to plan to pay for everything because that was her experience, whereas, Anthony felt it was important for the child to pay for his or her own education as he had. The key is to thoroughly discuss it to determine a plan and course of action.

4.   **Determine retirement objectives.**
     (a) When do you want to retire?
     (b) What does your retirement look like?
     (c) Do you want to live on less, equal, or more money in retirement than you did pre-retirement?
     (d) What type of standard of living do you desire?

5.   **Consider parents and inter-generational planning.**
     (a) Have your parents planned effectively for their future?
     (b) Will you be financially responsible for them? If you are thinking about marrying, or are currently married, this is especially critical to address.
     (c) What strategies exist for addressing this?

6. **Assess risk management strategies.**
    Strive to protect against financial loss in the event of a death, disability of the wage earner, theft, or accidental loss of real or personal property, unforeseen liabilities, etc. In other words, a thorough understanding of the appropriate types and amounts of insurance coverage is important.

7. **Assess asset protection strategies.**
    (a) The first step is doing everything you can to prevent the lawsuit. However, in today's society, lawsuits seem to be unavoidable. Therefore, in addition to maintaining appropriate levels of malpractice and liability coverage, you should investigate strategies to help protect your family from personal financial loss.
    (b) Are you in a position to consider more advanced planning strategies, such as trusts, offshore accounts, family limited partnerships, etc.?

8. **Consider housing expenses.**
    (a) How much should you spend on your home?
    (b) What tax efficiencies should be considered?
    (c) Will you be "house poor?"

9. **Become educated.**
    (a) *Books:* The top five percent of income earners in 2005 earned $136,000 or more. This top 5% pays 55% of the overall federal tax revenue for this country. Among the challenges for our clients, who make up this 5%, are high incomes, high net worth, desire for tax efficient wealth accumulation, and asset protection. When reading books published for the masses, review the information critically, and seek advice specialized to your situation. We have found with that for our clients, the information from most books about finances may not necessarily apply to their situations.
    (b) *Other Resources:* people seek advice from a variety of people. As with books, it is important to critically evaluate each person's level of expertise. If you were having a major surgery, chances are you would have a variety of specialists involved. The key is each specialist contributing where their specific skill set lies.

(i)   Financial Planner/Advisor—We will address this later in the book.

(ii) CPA—typically great at providing specific tax or tax planning advice. Definitely an important member of the team.

(iii) Attorney—the area of focus could include Asset Protection, Estate Planning, Trust Development (among others).

(iv) Family Member—perhaps a member of your family has financial success (maybe not) and provides advice. Is it specific to you and your situation? Is it up to date?

(c) *The Virtual Puzzle.* Pictures and anecdotes often make the information easier to understand. In many cases, advisors simply run basic calculations. This is a good starting point, but the problem with basic calculation is that the resulting plan is linear, allowing for little in the way of changes. Your individual goals are like the many pieces of a puzzle; as your goals change, the various pieces change, and subsequently the overall picture (THE PLAN) will change.

10. **Develop the blueprint and action plan.**

Once you have established your goals, it is time to develop the blueprint. This blueprint serves as the foundation upon which all planning is built; it illustrates how to achieve your desired outcome. There is a huge difference between a financial plan and "real life planning." No life experience is unswerving—often there are many hiccups and speed bumps. As such, your plan must have commitment and flexibility. Think of the action plan as a "to-do" list. When items are accomplished we check them off and as changes, expected or not occur we check those off later.

11. **Initiate the 20/20 Rule.**

First of all, we are not fond of general rules of thumb. However, through the years, one question surfaced time and time again from our clients: "Can you give me a general rule of thumb of how much I need to save?" Keeping in mind the uniqueness of each client's situation, we worked with our mentor, Shaun McDuffee to develop the 20/20 Rule. This general guideline for saving is: saving 20% of your gross income may in many cases position you to retire in 20 years. We establish a goal for all of our clients to carve out 20% of their income for savings (Pay Yourself First) before they increase their standard of living in an effort to help them achieve their goals on time. More on this in a moment.

12. **Implement the plan.**

   Maintain flexibility within a baseline. Begin with monthly savings/ investing of 20% of your gross income towards your goals; basic savings, portfolio development, college education funding, retirement, intergenerational planning, etc. Additional income is applied to new goals or opportunities.

13. **Monitor and adjust the plan.**

   Annual reviews facilitate communication about the changes in your goals, as well as family or work situations. In addition, it also presents an opportunity to determine whether adjustments to your financial plan or implemented strategies are appropriate.

IV

The 20/20 Rule

A. What it is: This rule is the foundation of becoming "lucky", or taking advantage of the opportunity available to you. In our practice, a majority of our doctors in training complete their program between the ages of 30–35. A corresponding majority express their desire to have the option to leave medical practice between the ages of 50–55. *Thus, the 20/20 Rule—save 20% of your gross income in excess of your contributory pre-tax plan to provide yourself the option to walk away in 20 years.*

B. Why it is used? This benchmark rule is a guideline used to establish how much to save. Visiting with an advisor will be necessary to determine which level of savings is appropriate for you and where these dollars will be allocated, as it will be different for each person based on their goals.

C. When to use it: The time to implement this strategy is immediately upon completion of training. For example, let's say you earn $40,000 while in training and upon completion your income is $250,000. How difficult would it be to live on $200,000? In over ten years, we have never had a client or their spouse suggest that living on $200,000 per year will be a challenge.

The following chart shows the projected earnings of the $50,000 yearly investment over 20 years at 6%, 8%, and 10%.

The Benefit of Compounding[1]

The following is an illustration of the growth of a $50,000 annual investment for 20 years at three different rates of return, with investments made in monthly increments of $4,167.

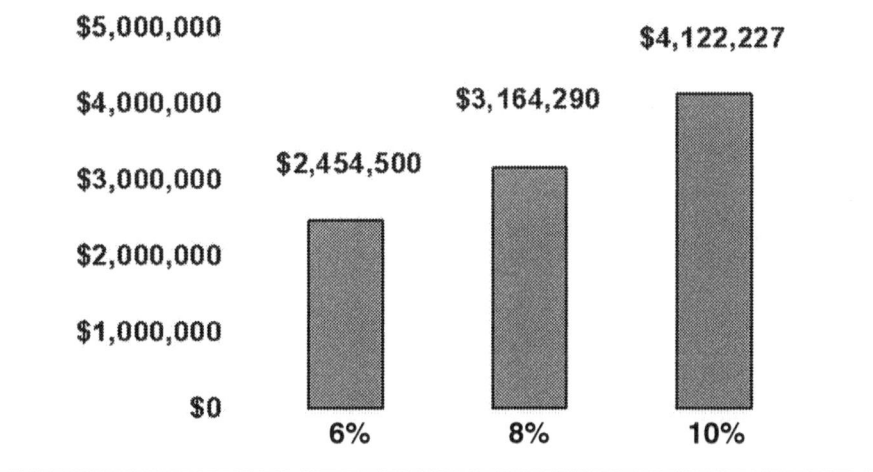

Investment Returns: A Long-Term Perspective[2]
Annual Compounded Returns

	Last 80 Years 1926 to 2005	Last 30 Years 1976 to 2005	Last 15 Years 1991–2005
Small Company Stocks	12.64%	17.55%	17.14%
Common Stocks (S&P 500)	10.36%	12.72%	11.52%
Long-Term Corp. Bonds	5.92%	9.55%	9.07%
Long-Term Gov't Bonds	5.47%	9.49%	9.41%
U.S. Treasury Bills	3.71%	6.05%	3.86%
Inflation Rate	3.04%	4.31%	2.61%

D. On the other hand, consider a client who has already been making $250,000 for some time. How likely is it that this client would carve out $50,000 for savings, investing, or anything else? In fact, we have a client earning $500,000 annually who struggles to save $1,500 per month–$18,000 per year. In a recent meeting, this client expressed frustration because he likely wouldn't hit his financial goals. We explained to him that he could reach his goals if he was willing to adjust his standard of living. As you can imagine, this was not a comfortable discussion for him and his wife, nor will it be an easy transition of their income allocation.

E. To further illustrate the power of starting to save early in your career:

The Cost of Waiting to Begin Investing[3]			
Here is the monthly investment required to accumulate $1,000,000 by age 65, assuming an average 10% compounded rate of return.			
Age to Begin Investing	25	35	45	55
Monthly Investment Amount to Reach Goal of $1 Million	$158	$442	$1,316	$4,882

The objective of the 20/20 Rule: to position yourself to take advantage of the opportunity of a sizeable income increase upon entering practice and ultimately to achieve your financial objectives. Now go make yourself lucky!

V

Does debt have you down?

The key to evaluating debt is your paradigm, or the lens through which you see things. In our experience people approach debt with two primary anchors: "**financial sensibility**" and "**emotional sensitivity**". *Financial sensibility* involves if you had extra money in your budget on a monthly basis, would you financially be better off if you applied the money towards debt or to savings/investment. *Emotional sensitivity* involves deep rooted discomfort, boarding on hatred for debt no matter what the interest rate. Now before we go further, one of the first steps is to open your student loan envelopes (you might be amazed how many doctors in training do not do this). Regardless of how depressing it may be, these numbers represent your investment in yourself and you should be proud. Moving on, we will discuss three types of debt: credit cards, student loans, and home loans.

A.   *Credit cards.*

In most cases, the emotional reaction to credit card debt is a different one than that toward other types of debt such as home or student loans. As a result of this strong emotional discomfort, we feel paying these off as quickly as possible is likely your best strategy. If you have credit card debt before establishing a savings/investment plan, we recommend paying the credit card debt out of the 20% of gross income set aside for savings. Once this credit card is gone, you are already in the habit of allocating the 20% and as such will have a fairly simple transition to savings/investing.

B.   *Student loans.*

From the "financial sensibility" perspective, with low student loan interest rates, it would often make sense to let your great-great grandchildren pay off your student loans. Of course, this isn't a true option, but it is the thought behind the concept of financial leverage.

Student Loan Example[4]

- *Loan amount of $100,000*
- *Consolidated at 3% interest rate.*
- *30 year payoff = $422 per month*
- *10 year payoff = $966 per month*
- *Difference in payments = $544 per month*

Option One: 30 year payoff plan, investing $544 difference each month.

Option Two: 10 year payoff plan, investing $0 for 10 years, then $966 for 20 years.

At the end of 30 years, here is the difference between Option One net worth minus Option Two net worth:

> At 8%—$241,758
> At 9%—$350,748
> At 10%—$496,158

Result—Not only is the net worth higher with Scenario One, but liquidity and budget flexibility are maintained. Imagine trying to go back to the student loan company after committing to the ten-year payment plan and asking to adjust the payment or asking for your money back! What would happen in the event of financial hardship if you had committed to the ten-year payment plan?

After presenting a similar example to one client having $250k of student loans at 5%, we received a much unexpected response. "One million dollars in thirty years does not mean more to me than $250,000 does today" (We illustrated the Option One Payment Plan from above at 10%). We immediately realized that the "emotional sensitivity" component of the paradigm far outweighed the "financial sensibility" component. We then asked the client a question, "What if, at the end of year five of your six year payback strategy (his proposal), what if you became financially debilitated? What if you could no longer earn an income? Could you go to your student loan carrier and ask for money back? Could you ask to have your payment lowered?" Here is the bottom line: if you were presented with a situation where your choice is to either default on your student loans or take care of your family, which would you choose?

Another consideration relating to student loans is to ensure that you obtain **written copies** of the promises made by any student loan consolidation counselor. Over the years we have seen too many instances where the presented arrangement is not actually what occurs. And without a copy of these specifics in writing, our client has no recourse.

C.   *Mortgages.*

First, let us say, there is no "right" way to manage this type of debt. But, the same principles covered earlier in relation to student loans may also apply exponentially to your home loan. As we mentioned previously, your financial situation is unique to the top 5% of income earners. So, from an income tax perspective, it may not make sense to pay your home off, as conventional wisdom might have you believe. Taxes are, or will be, the bane of your existence. Some of you, i.e. doctors in training, will soon pay more in taxes than what you currently earn. Others among you already experience this tax burden. One of the primary ways to lower your tax liability is the interest deduction you gain from owning a home. One way to maximize this interest deduction, lowering your overall income tax liability, is to leverage your house appropriately. The larger mortgage you carry, the larger your tax deduction. Two words of caution: this is not an excuse to overextend or become "house poor." Second, be mindful of the maximum limits for a mortgage acquisition debt and home equity loans. Mortgage interest in excess of those limits is not eligible for an income tax deduction. It is crucial to review current tax laws pertaining to mortgage interest. It is also important to confer with an in-state advisor who can determine the extent to which your home is protected in the event of litigation.

- Financially, paying off your mortgage may not be in your best interest for many reasons. It is important for each individual to evaluate their specific situation taking into consideration their goals, income, available interest rates, etc.
- Emotionally, your sensitivity towards debt is a strong component. But, consider what would happen if your income was lost through disability, or some other unforeseen crisis? Should financial debilitation occur, assets such as a mortgage-free home may be at risk if liquidity is needed for current expenses. At the same time, it may also be difficult to continue making mortgage payments without income coming in. Depending on which state you live in, state laws regarding mortgage debt may or may not assist your family in the event of judgments and/or foreclosures. Proper leveraging of mortgage debt should be carefully considered and reviewed when purchasing a home.

Another potential strategy, which uses the "financial sensibility" component, is to make the smallest possible down payment. The following example shows how two differing down payment scenarios affect net worth in various circumstances. When considering the example below, determine what is appropriate for your situation:

Home Mortgage Illustration

- Home Purchase Price: $100,000
- Person A: Is debt averse and pays cash
- Person B: Put 5% down, and invests $94,000
  - Takes out a $95,000 interest only mortgage
  - Pays $1,000 of mortgage acquisition costs
- Each person has $100,000 of capital available and has annual cash flow of $7,000 available
- Each person is in a 30% income tax bracket
- Housing values in the area appreciate 5% annually
- These are the only factors included in this analysis

Result after 1 year:

	Person A	**Person B**
Home Value	$105,000	$105,000
Amount owed on Mortgage	0	$(95,000)
Equity in Home	$105,000	$ 10,000
Invest capital at 8%	0	$101,520
Invest cash flow at 8%	$ 7,560	
Invest income tax savings		
From mortgage interest at 8%	0	$ 2,100
	$112,560	$113,620

Result after 5 years:

	Person A	**Person B**
Home Value	$127,628	$127,628
Amount owed on Mortgage	0	$(95,000)
Equity in Home	$127,628	$ 32,628
Invest capital at 8%	0	$138,117
Invest cash flow at 8%	$ 44,351	
Invest income tax savings		
From mortgage interest at 8%	0	$ 13,305
	$171,979	$184,050

Under this simplistic example, where the interest expense on the mortgage debt is less than the investment earnings on invested capital, Person B "comes out" ahead. But, keep in mind that Person B has taken on more risk. If investment earnings fall, any advantage to Person B would be eliminated. It is crucial for a home owner to thoroughly understand these risk/return issues and how their cash flow may be affected by a career interruption or long-term disability. You are advised to consult your tax professional when making these decisions.

The average specialist retires on 70–80% of their pre-retirement income, so most of them will enter retirement in a similar tax bracket as they experienced before retirement. Taking cash from investments to pay off the mortgage balance eliminates one of the last remaining tax breaks. This might not be in a high income earners best interest. Also, there are other factors to consider; children no longer live at home, no further 401k contributions are being made, and you will likely have no business deductions, taking away the most commonly used tax-saving strategies. Additionally, you must consider that your exposure to litigation does not diminish upon retirement. Having a huge chunk of equity in your home might expose you to potential legal threats depending on the state in which you live.

Your income and your potential for lawsuit are greater; therefore your strategy should be different. It is important to base your strategies on your unique facts and situation which is likely different from a majority of income earners.

VI

Investment Strategies & Investments

Nostradamus said there are things we cannot predict. Two such impossible predictions are whether the market will rise or fall and which sector of the market will perform well one year to the next. There are two strategies that help to alleviate the guesswork.

A. *Dollar Cost Averaging.*

This principle is based on the maxim, "Buy low and sell high." This strategy helps you successfully pursue the "buy low" portion of that maxim, by allowing you to buy shares of a security at a lower average cost than the average share price. The key to successful investing is a consistent disciplined automated approach.

For example, let's say you have $500 to invest over five months. One strategy is to place all the money into the investment immediately. Another strategy is to allocate the amount monthly. Over the five months, the share price goes from $10, $5, $2, $5, and $10. In the first strategy you would still have $500 at the end of five months. In the second strategy you would have $1100. The concept is to buy more shares when the price is low and buy fewer shares when the price is high. It's like shopping at Nordstrom's half-yearly sale: you can buy quality goods at a lower price.

For further illustration, consider the following example.

Dollar Cost Averaging[6]

Month Purchased	Investment Amount	Share Price	Shares Purchased
January	$1,000	$40	25
February	$1,000	$50	20
March	$1,000	$40	25
April	$1,000	$25	40
May	$1,000	$40	25
June	$1,000	$50	20
Totals:	$6,000		155

Average Share Price: $40.83
Your Average Cost per Share: $38.70
Difference/Savings per Share: $2.13

1. **Take emotions into account.** Often when people invest, fear and greed are their primary emotions. With the Dollar Cost Averaging approach you worry less about ebbs and flows of the market or when to buy or sell because you are investing on a systematic basis. You are as likely to invest when prices are low as when they are high.

2. **Market timing does not work.** Peter Lynch of Fidelity Investments and investor and CEO Warren Buffet have both spoken out against market timing, saying that success comes from time in the market rather than timing the market.

As you can see by the graph below, missing out on the best 30 months over an eighty year time frame dramatically impacts your growth.

Market Timing: An Expensive Strategy[7]
The Value of $1.00 Invested in 1926–2005

• Large Company Common Stocks $2657.56

• Large Company Common Stocks
  Minus the 30 Best Months $34.49

B.   *Asset Allocation.*

We do not have a crystal ball indicating which sector in the market will do well from one year to the next. With a consistently rebalanced portfolio, again we can lessen the emotional aspect of investing while maintaining the portfolio in line with your personal risk/tolerance profile.

Risk Reduction Illustration[8]
Example using date of October 19, 1987

Portfolio #1—   100% Stocks
  $10,000   Investment
  -2,300   Single Day Loss
  $7,700   **Remainder**

Portfolio #2—   50% Stocks/50% Bonds
  $10,000   Investment
  -1,150   Single Day Stock Loss
  8,850
  + 600   Single Day Bond Gain
  $9,450   **Remainder**

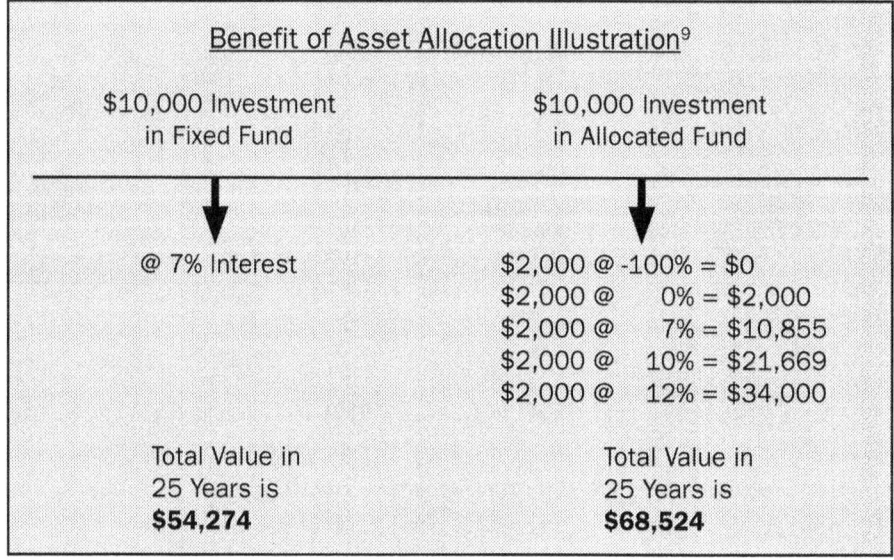

C. *Opportunity Cost*

1. One of the many challenges our clients face is that as their non-tax deferred investment portfolio grows, their tax liability increases. Often we are asked the following questions relating to the investment portfolio:
    (a) What is this 1099 DIV tax form we received? Or, if applicable, why did I receive one even in a down market?
    (b) Why am I paying extra taxes?
    (c) When will I ever use this money?

2. The real question should be, "What is the opportunity cost on the monies used to pay the tax?" In other words, what would the tax monies have grown too, if instead of paying taxes via the gains on this medium term portfolio had the monies stayed invested in a tax efficient environment?

D.   *Criteria of Investment Suitability*

The following are three criteria we often use to determine the appropriate vehicles for our clients to achieve their goals. In the next chapter we will discuss tax considerations as additional criteria.

1.   **Accessibility/Time Frame**. When deciding on which type of investment vehicle to pursue, it is important to determine how long you can afford to tie up the invested dollars. Remember that short-term investments are generally not appropriate for long-term objectives and vice versa. For example, a variable annuity, 401k, or individual stocks probably aren't appropriate for accomplishing short-term goals any more than a money market would be for a thirty-year investment time frame.

2.   **Risk/Volatility**. There are questionnaires and other tools available to aid in determining individual risk tolerance. Risk tolerance refers to how comfortable you are with market volatility. Can you tolerate watching your investment accounts go up and down with the market, but giving you an opportunity for higher returns? Or, are you more comfortable earning a fixed rate of return even if it is lower? It is important to match your portfolio with your individual tolerance.

3.   **Asset Protection**. Is the investment vehicle afforded statutory protection from potential judgments? Will you need to enhance your protection using other vehicles?

VII

Tax Efficiency and Growing your Net Worth

One of the primary considerations when growing your net worth is tax efficiency. Often people focus only on the present, when they should also consider the potential tax efficiency over time and into their retirement years.

A. *Bucket Strategy.*

All of your investments fit into three categories, or buckets.

1. **Fully taxable** investments require you to pay taxes on investment income earned and capital gains recognized each year. Examples: savings accounts, stocks, certain types of bonds, CDs or mutual funds.

    (a) *Mutual fund features*: Dollars are contributed after-tax. During the growth of the investment, annual distributions by the mutual fund are periodically taxed. In addition, any time you rebalance your portfolio, any gains on the shares sold are taxed (we generally will want to follow and asset allocation strategy, as well as avoid taxes which creates a conflict). Finally, when you cash out or sell your mutual funds you will pay tax on any gains which have not yet been taxed.

    (b) *Stock investment features*: Again, you will have a tax liability when you rebalance your portfolio and by selling stock realizing a gain. For active traders who rarely hold a stock for longer than a year, this tax is at their ordinary income tax rate. For stocks (and mutual funds), held longer than 12 months, gains on shares sold will be taxed as long-term capital gains. Currently that rate is 15% for federal income taxpayers in the 15% ordinary income tax bracket or higher.

2. **Tax-deferred** investment vehicles accumulate without recognition of tax liability. However, principal and gains are taxable upon withdrawal at ordinary income tax rates (whatever those might be at time of withdrawal). Examples include most qualified plans, such as, traditional IRAs, 401ks, SEPs, TSAs, defined contribution plans, and pension plans.

    (a) Pre-tax/tax-deferred investments' features: These dollars are contributed on a pre-tax basis, allowing you to lower your income tax liability today. The invested money grows tax-deferred (no tax liability while funds remain in the account), with the dollars taxed upon withdrawal.

    (b) Restrictions: If you access the accounts prior to age 59 ½, you will pay a 10% early withdrawal penalty (although some exceptions to this penalty may apply). Additionally, at age 70 ½, you are required to take "Required Minimum Distributions" from the account each year using one of the three IRS approved methods of calculation. Failure to take those distributions beginning after age 70 ½ can result in additional tax penalties.

3. **Tax-advantaged** investments grow tax-free and can provide tax-advantaged income. Examples: municipal bonds, cash values of life insurance, 529 plans, and Roth IRAs.

    (a) After tax/tax-advantaged investments' features: Dollars are contributed after-tax. The dollars grow tax-deferred while in the account. Taxation upon accessing the money varies by investment type. For instance, non-qualified annuity distributions of growth and interest are subject to tax while the cost basis in the annuity is received free of tax. Withdrawals from Roth IRA's can be received tax-free if it meets the definition of a qualified distribution. Cash values of life insurance can be accessed on a tax-advantaged manner through policy loans and withdrawals of basis.

Many of our clients come to us with too much in the fully taxable bucket, not enough in the tax-deferred bucket, and almost nothing in the tax-advantaged bucket. So the question we pose to you is, "Would you rather pay taxes on the seed or the harvest?"

B.   *Understanding Tax Brackets.*

The first step is to understand how tax brackets work. Often clients ask, "What tax bracket am I in?" Others make assumptions like the following: "I am in the 45% tax bracket." Or "I jumped into the next tax bracket this year." We once had a client who considered taking a contract with less pay because they felt their net income from the higher paying job would actually be lower after taxes. This is simply not true. The concept to understand is that federal income taxes are calculated on a graduated scale; taxpayers will have the benefit of lower rates on a portion of their income. (Note: This may not be true if you become subject to the Alternative Minimum Tax (AMT).

2007 Federal Tax Brackets and Rates[10]

Single	Rates	Married	Rates
$0 to $7,825	10%	$0 to $15,650	10%
$7,550–$31,850	15%	$15,650–$63,700	15%
$31,850–$77,100	25%	$63,700–$128,500	25%
$77,100–$160,850	28%	$128,500–$195,850	28%
$160,850–$349,700	33%	$195,850–$349,700	33%
Over $349,700	35%	Over $349,700	35%

As you can see by the tax table, for a married household, if you have an annual adjusted gross income of $400,000 (and if you are not subject to the AMT), the entire $400,000 is not exposed to 35%, only the taxable income above $336,550. So, from a financial planning perspective, it is important to identify how much your last dollars earned are being taxed, since that is where the tax-savings will have the most impact. In this example, $63,450 in income would be taxed at the highest bracket, 35%.

C.   *Controlling Your Money.*

Our goal for our clients is for them to have control over their money no matter what happens to tax rates. We know tax laws, including tax rates and income brackets, change year to year. This is why it is so important to have exposure to a variety of investments with different tax treatment. Frankly, even if taxes were to remain the same over time, your unique financial situation (high incomes, with high tax brackets, and exposure to litigation) alone makes diversification important. You must also consider the tax ramifications you will face in the future. For example, those of the Baby Boomer generation tend to be poor savers. By their sheer numbers, they have generated significant federal income taxes revenue for this country. However, as they move into retirement, their standard of living is project to be lower, thus, generating less tax revenue for the country. Additionally, as physicians, you know that $1 of every $5 per household is spent on healthcare costs. As people age the likelihood of increased health care costs is almost certain. What does this have to do with taxes? Think of a business facing both declining revenues and increasing expenses. Do the math and only one conclusion comes to mind—expect higher taxes.

D.   *Tax Diversification Example*

- Parameters: Client A has all their retirement savings in tax-deferred plans such as 401ks, SEP IRAs, etc. Client B has an even balance between tax-deferred investments and tax-advantaged plans such as cash values of permanent life insurance. Both clients currently earn $200,000 and both wish to transition to part-time employment at age 55. At age 55 both wish to cut their work hours and income in half while keeping their standard of living at $200,000. For this example, imagine that there are only two tax brackets: $0 - $100,000 = 25% tax and $100,001 - $200,000 = 50% tax.
- At Age 55: Client A will earn $100,000 and withdraw $100,000 from their tax-deferred plans, paying tax on $200,000. Client B will earn $100,000 and pull $100,000 from their tax-advantaged accounts utilizing tax-free policy loans, paying tax on only $100,000.
- At age 60: Both clients enter full retirement and wish to keep their standard of living at $200,000. Client A will withdraw $200,000 annually from

their tax-deferred accounts. $100,000 will be taxed at 25% and $100,000 will be taxed at 50% for a marginal (overall) tax liability of 37.5%. Client B will withdraw $100,000 from their tax-deferred account at a 25% tax rate, and $100,000 from their tax-advantaged account at a 0% tax rate, for a marginal tax liability of 12.5%.

- As a result, Client B maintains the flexibility to adjust retirement distribution strategies as tax environments change throughout retirement. Whereas Client A is limited to fully taxable distributions at all times.

- Conclusion: Though this is only a simplistic example, it illustrates that diversification of the tax treatment in the investment vehicle selected is critical to the planning process. Your financial plan will be subject to different tax brackets, more complex challenges and opportunities, as well as frequent changes. As a result, it is important to recognize the benefits of diversification, which you will reap both before and during retirement.

VIII

Debunking Three Common Tax Myths

Here are three of the most common presumptions about retirement that many people make, usually supported in general literature on the subject.

- **Myth #1: You will be in a lower tax bracket when you retire.** Conventional wisdom suggests it is always better to push taxes into the future because you are likely to be in a lower tax bracket, due to a reduction in income after retirement. Do you want "lower income" in retirement? We know better than to hope that Congress will reduce the tax rates. Most of our clients will be in a similar or potentially higher tax bracket during retirement so we must plan accordingly.

- **Myth #2: You will not need as much money in retirement to maintain your current standard of living.** In over 13 years, we have never had a client suggest that they would like to have a reduced standard of living during retirement. Taking into consideration variables such as inflation, travel, and rising health care costs to name a few, it will likely cost more to maintain the same standard of living.

- **Myth #3: Your investments, assuming an average rate of return, would grow in a straight line.** The key here is to realize the market has historically experienced huge swings. *When* these swings occur will greatly impact your retirement income. As such, tax efficient investing is critical to your success.

In this publication, we cannot begin to scratch the surface of the tax issues that pertain to qualified retirement distributions. According to a 2006 article in *Forbes* magazine, the average savings in 401k accounts for people age 59 and older is $97,000. What is the balance in your 401k? It is likely higher than the average retiree, and you probably have quite a while longer to contribute. How much will it be worth by age 59? Clients often tell us that everyone tells them to max out their 401k account. Or, they wonder why they haven't heard more about using cash value life insurance. Our experience is due to the uniqueness of our clients' situation, many magazine articles, books, and other publications which are often directed towards the masses may not apply to your situation. The bottom line is to make sure to diversify your tax exposure utilizing a variety of investment vehicles.

IX

Asset Protection Considerations

Asset protection laws are determined by each state. The first step is to visit with a financial advisor and local counsel to evaluate the legal ramifications of using various investments or business arrangements. In some states, the investment vehicle itself has been provided with asset protection features under the state statutes. In other instances, you may consider implementing legal entities such as an LLC, LLP, FLP, FST, PA, or PC might be considered. Depending on the client circumstances, structuring asset protection vehicles outside the country might be considered. It is critical to consult an attorney license in your state of residence who is experienced in this area of the law, to assist you in determining which strategy is appropriate for you and ensure that appropriate tax filing are made.

X

Employment Considerations

- *Your paradigm*: Your perspective on the interviewing process is a primary factor. For example, we counsel our clients to take the approach that they are interviewing the employer rather than the employer interviewing them. It is surprising how many people overlook the fundamental principle of protecting their interests.

- *Attorney review:* It is very important to have an attorney review your employment contracts to determine the potential for conflicts or misunderstandings over provisions.

- *Fair Market Value*: Review the contracts to determine fair market value of the proposed income and be sure to compare multiple offers. The income amount should be compared to other groups in the same specialty and geographic area.

- *Perks*: Are there any sign-on bonuses or moving allowances? Are they comparable to other groups in the area? If offered, ask to have these funds released to you as soon as possible.

- *Speak to a partner.* Invite the person who was just made partner out for coffee or lunch. Find out if they experienced any surprises or if, in hindsight, they have any questions they wish they had asked. Ask them if they like the other people with whom they work. An inside perspective is valuable in helping you to weigh your decision.

- *Non-Compete Clause:* Examine how the clause is structured and understand when it applies. Become aware of any possible financial repercussions you should expect if, in the future, your practice is found to be in violation of this clause.

- *Salary or Income payment:* Identify and evaluate how your income is to be determined—by billing, collections, patients, etc.

- *Tail coverage:* Determine the structure of your tail coverage. You should know whether or not you would have to pay for this coverage if you left the employer. If so, find out how that amount is determined. Additionally, identify how you would be protected in the event of a lawsuit against the group after your departure.

- *Nose Coverage:* Find out if this coverage is available and how it is structured.

- *Buy-in:* Determine the structure of buy-in. Ask questions pertaining to the amount, how it is paid (for example, is it a lump sum, part of a quarterly bonus, or some other structure)?

- *Partnership:* Questions to ask should include:
    1. What is the time frame for prospective partnership?
    2. How are partners paid?
    3. Is there a separate formula used to determine individual pay?
    4. After taking on expenses will your pay go up or down?
    5. Perhaps ask to review the Profit and Loss, if you are joining a smaller group without a public or proven track record of profitability.

- There are a variety of questions to consider. The key is to get everything in writing!

XI

Disability Insurance Coverage

Most individuals take the time to insure their homes, autos, boat, and other tangible assets against loss. But many fail to realize that their ability to earn an income is the most significant asset they have. If you lose the ability to work, due to an accident or long-term illness, your income will stop, yet your expenses for yourself and your family continues. Protecting your income in the event of a long-term disability should not be overlooked when addressing your financial security.

Disability Insurance coverage can be used to address this risk. Some policy features to consider:

- Disability policies may be issued on an individual or group basis. Policies are also available through associations and professional organizations.
- Benefit periods can vary from 24 month, 60 months, to age 65 or age 67. The longer period is recommended in most cases.
- "Non-cancelable" and "guaranteed renewable" are important provisions to look for in a disability income policy. These provisions mean that the insurance company cannot raise your rates or discontinue your coverage as long as you continue to pay your premiums.
- Elimination or waiting periods typically range from 30 days to one year. This is the length of time you must wait until policy benefits are paid. Longer elimination periods result in lower premium cost.
- Cost of living adjustments protect against inflation.
- Future benefits based on income only (not medical) are highly beneficial.
- The definition of disability is covered in more detail upcoming.

Other types of Disability Income Insurance policies include:

- Key Employee Disability Insurance—An employer may own a policy issued on a key employee. If the key employee becomes disabled, the policy benefits can be used to pay expenses related to the loss of services of that employee, such as hiring a replacement.
- Disability Buy-out—If a business owner or professional becomes disabled, these policy benefits can be used to satisfy the buy-out provisions of a Buy-Sell agreement.
- Business Overhead Expense—If a business owner or professional becomes disabled, it may be difficult to keep the business or practice running without their involvement. This type of policy can be used to provide funds to pay the on-going expense of the business, so it can continue functioning during a period of disability.

Of Special Note: There are many differences in policy provisions between different insurers and even between different contract forms from the same provider. Some policies do not require a complete disability, but pay benefits when an insured's earning drop by a certain percentage due to a disability. Some providers require a physician's certification to pay or to continue paying benefits. There are policies that provide for partial or residual benefits; for example, where the insured is not able to perform all the duties of his/her profession, but could perform some duties. Policy definitions and provisions should be carefully reviewed to ensure your policy will meet your financial needs and circumstances.

The key to private disability insurance is identifying your most valuable asset. In this case, think about an asset bigger than your home, car, or your financial statements. YOU are your most valuable asset—specifically, your skill set, which ultimately provides your ability to earn income. You have worked very hard for many years getting to this point. The last thing you would want to happen is to become disabled without having proper coverage, causing you to forfeit the income for which you have worked so hard.

A.   *Definitions.*

There are a variety of different definitions so I will list the most common here

- **"Double Dip Own Occupation"**, (also may be called "True Own Occupation", or "Pure Own Occupation"): Disability is defined as a condition which prevents you from performing the material and substantial duties of your specialty. Even if you are able to work in another capacity, you will still collect the disability income as a non-working specialist *in addition to* the income from the other job. This applies regardless of whether or not your new job is in medicine.
- **"Transitional Occupation"**: Like the previous type, if you cannot perform the material and substantial duties of your specialty you are considered disabled. However, if you earn an income, your total disability benefit will be proportionally reduced based on the amount of income earned from the new job (total new income disability benefit not to exceed previous earned income).
- **"Own Occupation"** or **"Regular Occupation"**: Again, if you cannot perform the material and substantial duties of your specialty you are considered disabled. You will only collect your disability benefit so long as you do NOT earn any income AND are under the constant care and supervision of a physician.

In our opinion, "Double Dip Own Occupation" disability coverage is the strongest definition and will best protect you and your family. Of course, it will still be important to evaluate which type of coverage is best for you. For instance, some contracts feature the "double dip own occupation" benefit for a limited time, usually between 24 and 60 months. Statistics indicate that if you are disabled for a period of two years or longer, you will most likely suffer ongoing disability for the remainder of your life. This is why a limited time frame for this benefit is not recommended in most cases.

B.   *Cost.*

The cost, or premium, will vary as it depends on your specialty and the various options you might elect to add to your coverage.

C.   *Benefit Amount.*

Another consideration is the amount of benefit you can actually receive. Often this requires combining policies from two or three companies in order to maximize the benefit. For example, some companies will offer $10,000 or $15,000 per month in benefit but will participate, or allow you to get additional coverage from another carrier in addition to what they offer, up to $20,000.

D.   *Timing.*

If you are in training, you should consider purchasing private disability insurance prior to entering practice. Consider these compelling reasons:

- While in training you can receive discounts on your premiums. This discount often carries forward, applying to future increases of benefit. Over time, this could amount to a significant savings for you.

- As is true with all insurance, premiums are based on age. The younger you are, the less risk you present to the insurer, hence lower premiums. So, your premiums will be less while you are in training. People often ask how much of a premium increase they can expect by waiting one year or more to begin coverage. Typically premiums increase approximately 10%–13% per year barring an unusual development in the disability insurance industry.

- Another significant consideration is the possibility of being offered group disability coverage upon entering practice. Besides being chosen and controlled by someone else, group coverage often has more limited definitions, such as "Any Occupation." In other words, if you relied on this type of group disability coverage, and due to disability could not perform your specialty but could work at any other job, you would not be considered disabled and would not receive any benefits.

- Key Point: If you have private coverage in training, and upon employment, your group offers you disability coverage; your group coverage will stack on top of your private coverage. This ultimately covers a higher percentage of your income. If you wait and take the group coverage and then decide to purchase private coverage, the private carrier will likely provide very little, if any, in the way of extra coverage as they will say you already have 60% of your income covered by the group policy. This is why it is imperative to purchase private disability insurance prior to joining a group. One strategy we utilize for our clients already in practice is to determine if they can opt out of their group coverage. This way they can obtain the private policy that will cover a higher percentage of their income. Finally, the reality is that for many of you, the group you join immediately out of training will not be the group with whom you practice for the remainder of your career. For all of these reasons, relying on group disability insurance is a risky proposition.

E. *One final note about disability insurance.*

The disability insurance industry has undergone massive changes in the past twenty years. Some of your older colleagues likely have private disability insurance that would replace 100% of their income for the rest of their lives. Most new policies replace 50–60% of your income until you reach age 65 or 67. We know of only one company still offering lifetime benefits, and at a much higher cost than in the past. Since industry changes are rarely in favor of the insured, it is recommended that you acquire the maximum benefit as soon as possible.

XII

Life Insurance Coverage

There are many different types of life insurance to consider. Because evaluating life insurance involves a variety of components, we will review the types of life insurance available first, then discuss an approach you may take in evaluating and purchasing life insurance.

Decreasing Term
The premium remains the same while the death benefit decreases.

Annual Renewable Term
The premium will increase on an annual basis while the death benefit remains the same.

Level Term
The premium remains the same for a specified period of time; 5, 10, 15, or 20 years, while the death benefit remains the same.

Cash Value—Ordinary Life or Whole Life
The premiums and death benefit remain the same while accumulating cash value on a tax-deferred basis. The uses of this type of life insurance include providing paying off debt, survivor income, and paying estate taxes.

Universal Life

The premiums and death benefit are flexible while accumulating cash value on a tax-deferred basis. The benefits and uses are very similar to Whole Life while providing an opportunity for enhanced cash value accumulation.

Variable Life

The premiums and death benefit may be adjusted, while accumulating cash value on a tax-deferred basis. The accumulation is directly impacted by market performance, specifically the type of investment option chosen; such as stock funds, bond funds, money market funds, etc.

Single Premium Life

One premium is paid at issue of contract with a level minimum death benefit while accumulating cash value.

First to Die

The premium may adjust while maintaining a minimum level death benefit on two or more parties. The death benefit is received at the first death.

Survivorship Life

The premium may adjust while maintaining a minimum level death benefit on two people. The death benefit is paid at the second death.

Mutual funds and Variable Products are sold through registered representatives only and must be accompanied by a prospectus. Read the prospectus carefully prior to investing or sending money.

Due to the various types of policies, each with a different approach to fulfilling one's needs for life insurance, it is important to evaluate and choose carefully. Key considerations include;

- Duration of the need
- Budget available
- Purpose for the need
- Attitude about life insurance policies
- Issues involved finding the best "short-term price" versus considerations of lowest "long-term cost."

- Age
- General health
- Tax advantages
- Liquidity at death
- Family Benefits

We recommend taking the following approach to life insurance: First, determine if there is a *need* for the insurance by identifying any financial loss that would occur in the event of your death. Examples of "financial loss" can include replacing the income of the family's wage earner(s), replacing the value of services provided to the family by a spouse not working outside the home, paying off a mortgage, paying final expenses, providing for college funds to name a few. The next step is to determine your *desires*. For example, in addition to providing for your family's survivor income needs, you may also wish to address estate planning concerns, retirement, charitable bequests, or leave a legacy for your family. Because of the complexity involved in these decisions, thorough discussion with your financial advisor is recommended.

XIII

Other Insurance Coverage

A. *Personal Liability Umbrella Insurance*

    1.   Purchasing a Personal Liability Umbrella Policy is an inexpensive way to address potential liability issues not covered by other insurances.

    2.   Some common real-life examples include:
- (a) A doctor's car backs up into an unseen pedestrian, causing bodily harm or property damage.
- (b) A gathering is hosted at a doctor's home with alcoholic beverages served. A guest is over-served and is involved in an auto accident.
- (c) A child attending a birthday party trips and falls on the doctor's property.

B. *Auto/Home Insurance*

Making sure to visit with your P & C (Property & Casualty) Agent to determine the appropriate coverage limits is critical to protect your home, vehicle, and personal items.

Let us offer a word about deductibles. As your net worth grows, consider raising your deductibles to save money on your monthly premium while self-insuring the deductible amount.

XIV

Type of Practice Best for You

This is arguably one of the most important decisions you face as you complete training. Should I open my own practice, join a specialty group, join a large scale hospital/corporate practice, or go academic and become an attending?

Often the primary consideration in this decision is quality of life. Many of our clients have entrepreneurial aspirations and opening their own practice is highly desirable. For the past years they have worked tons of hours and have no challenge continuing that. Others might wish to join a hospital or academic institution, realizing that they may not make as much, but won't have to work as much either.

Income, time, and running a business are other considerations to evaluate. What amount of time do you want to spend on your practice? Do you want to have to handle the business aspects of the business, e.g. payroll, staffing, benefits, etc? These factors may lead you to open your own practice or join an existing practice.

Visiting with other doctors already established in their practice (whichever path they chose) along with professional advice will assist you towards making the decision best for you.

XV

Financial Planners— Qualities to Seek

There are a number of issues to consider and a ton of information to sort through as you move down the path towards financial independence. Do you want to spend your time researching information, developing strategies, implementing vehicles, and constantly coordinating all the efforts of investment, tax, and legal advice? A financial planner can guide you through the process, ultimately saving you valuable time and effort in coordinating these elements.

✓ Personality: First and foremost, it is critical that you feel comfortable with the advisor. This will potentially be a long-term relationship, so establishing a good relationship with someone you trust is very important.

✓ Independent: It is critical to work with someone who can provide objective financial advice and has serving your best interests as their objective.

✓ Specialist: You should be able to answer "yes" to each of the following questions: Do they understand where you've been, where you are, and where you're going? Do they work exclusively with specialty doctors? Do they have a firm grasp of your desire not only to create wealth, but to protect it as well?

✓ Fee Planner: The advisor should charge a fee for financial planning and investment advice. We have found that working with this type of planner is more likely to result in objective and unbiased advice. Types of services provided by fee planners can vary, and are specified in a financial planning agreement.

XVI

Conclusion: Get Started

The first step is to take control of your finances. What happens if I have no money? Start by thinking about what could happen to your net worth by doing without a coffee, drink, lunches or dinners out. Then expand your thinking from there! Next, find the appropriate people to assist you in these endeavors and develop a comprehensive course of action. This is your call to action. Be proactive! Begin the process! Be "lucky!"

Notes

[1] Source: Small Company Stocks—represented by the fifth capitalization quintile of stocks on the NYSE for 1926–1981 and the performance of the Dimensional Fund Advisors (DFA) Small Company Fund thereafter; Large Company Stocks—Standard & Poor's 500, which is an unmanaged group of securities and is considered to be representative of the stock market in general; Corporate Bonds—are represented by the Salomon Brothers Long-Term High Grade Corporate Bond Index Government Bonds—20 year U.S. Government Bonds; Treasury Bill—30-day U.S. Treasury Bill; Inflation—Consumer Price Index.

[2-9] Source: Slides from Securian Advisor Website

[10] Source: 2007 IRS Tax Book

North Star Resource Group

Marathon Advisors, Inc.
Registered Investment Advisor

Anthony C. Williams, ChFC, CLU, RFC
Investment Advisor Representative

Marc E. Ortega, ChFC, RFC
Investment Advisor Representative

4645 N. 32nd Street #200
Phoenix, Arizona 85018
800.333.3366
602.224.5366
aw@northstarfinancial.com
marc.ortega@northstarfinancial.com

This book has provided information on various financial topics as well as investments. Keeping in mind that everyone's financial situation is different, the strategies and concepts discussed within this book may not be appropriate for everyone. You should meet with your financial, legal and tax advisor(s) before implementing any financial, legal or tax strategy.

The tax concepts that are addressed in this book are current as of 2007. Tax laws change frequently, and any tax concept addressed in this book may not be applicable after 2007.

Variable Life insurance, Variable Annuities and Mutual Funds are sold only by prospectus. The prospectus contains important information about the product's charges and expenses, as well as the risks and other information associated with the product. You should carefully consider the risks, investment charges of a specific product before investing. You should always read the prospectus carefully before investing.

Anthony C. Williams and Marc E. Ortega are investment advisor representatives with Marathon Advisor, Inc., a Registered Investment Advisor. They do not provide specific tax advice. Please consult with a tax professional before implementing any strategy.

2007 0564 MA1
DOFU 3/1/2007

About the Authors

Anthony C. Williams, ChFC, CLU

Senior Partner;* Financial Advisor for Physicians
President, Medical Division

office   (602) 224-5366
fax   (602) 224-9044
e-mail   anthony.williams@northstarfinancial.com
website www.northstarfinancial.com

Anthony provides specialty physicians and their families with strategies to accumulate and protect wealth for increased financial freedom. For over ten years, Anthony has worked with doctors through the Western United States addressing their unique issues.

- Debt Management
- Insurance Planning[2]
- Asset Protection
- Tax Minimization[1]
- Wealth Accumulation

Anthony is a Chartered Financial Consultant (ChFC), Chartered Life Underwriter (CLU), and Registered Financial Consultant (RFC). He is a featured keynote speaker on issues pertinent to specialists groups and teaching hospitals throughout the West. Anthony currently serves as President of North Star's Specialty Medical Division. He is a graduate of Arizona State University Business School.

His mission is to make a difference in people's lives. This value fuels his passion for what he does and sets him apart as a financial advisor. He is gratified by clients who trust and respect him and are delighted with his services.

"Each client is uniquely important. The relationships I develop are long term and mutually beneficial. The trust and respect created allows me to challenge my clients to make the difficult decisions needed to achieve financial freedom. My clients appreciate uncompromising integrity."

Anthony serves in many capacities with Stepping Stones of Hope; a non-profit organization assisting children and their families having experienced the death of a loved one. He is a past board member, current Camp Director for Camp Erin, and volunteer for Camp Paz. Anthony enjoys spending time with his wife, Wendy, a RN and his Weimaraner, Tempest.

[1] *Specific tax and legal consequences should be verified by your tax advisor and legal counsel.*

Marcus E. Ortega, ChFC, RFC

Financial Advisor for Physicians, Senior Partner*

office   (602) 224-5366
fax   (602) 224-9044
e-mail   marc.ortega@northstarfinancial.com
website   www.northstarfinancial.com

Marc provides specialty physicians and their families with strategies to accumulate and protect wealth for increased financial freedom. He believes in a proactive, preventative approach, similar to his clients' view of preventative medicine. Since 1994, Marc has worked with physicians addressing their unique issues.

- **Wealth Accumulation**
- **Asset Protection**
- **Tax Minimization**
- **Insurance Planning**
- **Debt Management**

Marc is a Chartered Financial Consultant (ChFC), Registered Financial Consultant (RFC) and a founding member of the North Star Medical Division. He has also been distinguished by the Million Dollar Round Table (MDRT), The Premier Association of Financial Professionals® recognizing the top 5 percent of financial advisors worldwide, as one of the industries leading advisors.

Marc's mission statement sums up his view on his career:

"I believe that balance is imperative in people's personal and financial life. My impact on my clients extends beyond their financial success. I give my clients vision and aim to be their trusted advisor to coach them through all of their financial needs."

Marc resides in Mesa, AZ with his wife, Deidra and children, Jayden and Marcus.

978-0-595-43913-3
0-595-43913-6